Work Freely

Love your job

Love your life

Nancy Richardson &
Rochelle Davidson

Work

Freely

ISBN 978-1-9991879-0-3 (paperback)
ISBN 978-1-9991879-1-0 (ebook)

Published by AsianDragonLady Productions

Produced by Page Two
www.pagetwo.com

Cover design by Kristine Arth
Interior design by Taysia Louie and Fiona Lee
Interior illustrations by Fiona Lee

www.workfreely.co

"IT TAKES COURAGE TO

GROW UP AND BECOME

WHO YOU REALLY ARE."

E.E. CUMMINGS

CONTENTS

THIS BOOK
IS FOR *YOU*

THE CONCEPT OF this book is *choosing* your life instead of letting it choose you. All too often, we are consumed by trying to fit into someone else's box, going from one job to the next, one manager to the next, one project to the next, only to realize that years, and maybe even decades, have gone by in the pursuit of achieving a life we "hoped" would someday become a reality. *Work Freely* is about flipping the script and taking the time to lay out your goals, dreams, and aspirations—designing your career to suit you—then choosing the companies, bosses, friends, and other circumstances that meet the criteria you've set, to live and work with ultimate freedom. This book is about choosing your path, defining your leadership, and finding your power to make a life you love not just a possibility but a sure thing.

In the pages ahead, you'll find a series of stories, each followed by personal coaching by my very own longtime executive coach, Rochelle Davidson. My stories reflect the career challenges I have faced that have kept me from feeling free in the workplace. Coaching is what helped me overcome these obstacles. As you read Rochelle's coaching sections ("Get Coached to Work Freely"), envision that you're in a session with her, having an intimate discussion that involves all of your senses, in a time just for you. The lessons I share in my stories, combined with Rochelle's coaching commentary, are designed to equip you with the tools to manage adversity, accelerate your career, and access your Super Self. (See chapter 10.)

This book is meant to be read right before bed, on vacation, or whenever you need to calm a busy mind. It is a tool to help you relax, take back control of your life circumstances, and embrace the fact that "you cannot fail, you can only learn." I hope that you can relate to the stories, personally benefit from the coaching, and know that you are never alone. Read the chapters in any order you like, feeling free to jump around and choose those that are most relevant to you, at the times in your life when you need them the most.

NANCY RICHARDSON

Get Coached

Working beside Nancy in an executive coaching capacity, I am constantly inspired by her courage to look herself in the mirror in service of becoming the leader, mother, wife, and friend she knows she is. That Nancy is willing to so openly share her journey and her lessons is a gift to all of us.

As your coach throughout these pages, I will be your thought partner, cheerleader, ass kicker, and collaborator. You are the expert in your life and I am a fierce stand for what you want, holding that vision even when you are not able to. I don't tell you what you need to do. That's up to you. As a coach, I ask you questions—sometimes inspiring, sometimes really frustrating—with the goal of deepening your learning and activating those areas that are most important for you.

In today's complex and uncertain times, the world needs leaders like Nancy and like you. You are conscious leaders who want to be your best, design your path, learn from experience, lean into challenges, and ultimately have big impacts. It's not about taking the easy road; it is about doing what's right—for yourself, your team, your family, your community—and in that there is a sense of freedom. The ripple effect is significant. The world becomes a better place.

ROCHELLE DAVIDSON

1

CHOOSE

YOUR LIFE

01

DRAGON LADY

Declare Who You Are Not, Discover Who You Are

There are almost as many definitions of what it means to be a leader as there are people working on leadership. How must you show up so that you inspire others to follow, regardless of your position or title? Trying to fit into one of the established definitions of leadership competency rarely works! When you figure out who you are at your core, have the humility to accept who you are not, and act from this place of authenticity, people will follow—and you will leave your mark on the world.

It was May 2010. I was beginning my new job at lululemon as the director of digital guest experience. In my first few weeks on the job, it was apparent that I was not at Starbucks anymore. I'd like to say I'm someone who makes decisions and never looks back. But boy did I spend a lot of time wondering if I had made the right decision. Had I been crazy to leave? Where would I be if I had stayed? I knew that looking backward would not help me move forward, but I was struggling with the choice I had made.

The Starbucks Support Center in Seattle, Washington, employed four thousand employees and more than 200,000 partners worldwide. The Support Center was four stories high, beautifully remodeled, with glossy wood floors connecting each wing of the building and a kitchen in every corner of each floor, where you could make your perfect Starbucks beverage at any time of the day. The building housed comfortable couches and big cozy chairs for casual meetings, a large cafeteria with a diverse menu, and a gym with classes and equipment you could access all day long.

The lululemon office, on the other hand, had fewer than two hundred employees and only a few thousand in their stores across North America. The building was old, although it had character—not the beautiful design and architecture of the Starbucks building but a gritty, sweaty environment that bled hard work and perseverance. They didn't have comfy chairs, a cafeteria, or a gym. This company and its people were on a mission; they were determined and focused on greatness. No bells and whistles here.

I was given a desk in the middle of the room with the other directors. I did not sit with my team. I had a hierarchical mentality and thought that I was smart, I knew what I was doing, I had successfully done this work at Starbucks, and my team should listen to me and do as I said. I was a Smart Boss. (See chapter 2.)

Long story short, this type of mentality did not go over very well at lululemon.

I wanted to be liked and respected, but I didn't know how to lead in this new environment, until one particular day changed the trajectory of my career forever and put me on the path of becoming a true leader.

It was Friday and, wanting to do something nice for my new team, I brought in pastries from Starbucks. I still didn't know my team very well, and I thought this would be a great opportunity to casually get to know them. I laid the pastries out individually in separate bags on my desk and then happily sent an email informing my team that "I brought pastries... They're on my desk. All you have to do to get one is swing by and say hello."

The pastries sat on my desk all day. No one came.

Finally, at the end of the day, one of the managers on my team stopped by my desk on her way out. Carolyn was a wicked-smart, strong, friendly, and powerful force inside the company. She was the manager at the time and had started the digital marketing team on her own. She had long, dark brown hair, the bluest eyes, and a gorgeous, bright white smile. Her demeanor was confident and

"

Changing a deep-rooted habit like my leadership style would be like training for a marathon, requiring daily commitments that, over time, would result in a monumental shift from my current paradigm.

"

humble. She respectfully approached me with an important message that I badly needed to hear.

She came around to my side of the desk, still standing, and quietly whispered, "You know, the reason no one is coming by for pastries is because they're scared of you. Your nickname on the floor is 'Asian Dragon Lady.'"

I'm half Chinese, so I suppose the first part of the name was accurate... but *Dragon Lady*?

At home that night, I told my husband, Sean, what happened. I expected him to balk at Carolyn's feedback. On the contrary, he looked at me with a compassionate, loving smile, leaned in, and said, "We call you that at home too."

I was blown away. I believe there is always *some* truth in feedback, but could *this* be true?

Every day, I struggled to make it home on time to see my kids. When I worked at Starbucks, I was out the door by 5 a.m. and home after dark, just barely in time to read them a bedtime story and put them to sleep, only to log back on to work until midnight.

I did this for the first ten years of my career. I felt I needed to put in my ten thousand hours. I was never the smartest person in school, a B-average at best. And to compensate for this, I believed needed to develop a superhuman work ethic. I was determined to be successful but felt I needed to work twice as hard as everyone else in order to make it.

This standard of work led to promotions and job opportunities; however, it caused me to be severely lacking in other areas of my life, specifically in my marriage and parenting. I was so enveloped in work—totally focused on getting ahead, getting promoted, and advancing in my field—that I ultimately became numb to the reason I was doing all this: my purpose in life.

My first step was to write down my personal and professional goals. They needed to be simple, tangible, daily commitments that were realistic and achievable. My personal goals were the following:

- Be home for dinner every night.
- Make dinner myself, twice a week.
- Read to my children each night before bed.
- Have a date night with my husband once a week.

Professionally, I would

- allow others to contribute,
- get curious and ask questions,
- be compassionate and seek to understand where people are coming from,
- stay calm and make sure people feel comfortable in my presence, and
- be a coach, not a dictator.

"

I became fiercely
committed to
becoming someone
people follow because
they *want to*, not
because they *have to*.

"

Each day consisted of small commitments, and, little by little, people started to migrate to me. I was friended on Facebook and invited to workouts and end-of-day drinks with the team. And on my birthday that year, I received a handwritten card from my daughter that read:

Dear Momma,

Thank you for teaching me how to swim and float on my back!! I think you are the best momma because you teach me new things and help me learn!!

Your loving daughter, Kaia Malia

This was the ultimate payoff and solidified my purpose. Learning this lesson at thirty-four years old was the beginning of a new era.

Today, acting like my inner Asian Dragon Lady is the exception, not the rule. And yet the nickname is always in the back of my mind as a gentle reminder of the type of leader I choose not to be.

Get Coached to Work Freely

What type of leader do you want to be? What do you want to be known for? What will your legacy be? Through a lot of personal reflection and the gift of generous feedback

"IF YOU'RE GOING
TO LIVE, LEAVE
A LEGACY. MAKE
A MARK ON THE
WORLD THAT CAN'T
BE ERASED."

MAYA ANGELOU

"

Knowing who you are,
and who you are not,
is fundamental to
defining your legacy.

"

from Carolyn and Sean, Nancy was able to define who she wanted to be—as a mother, wife, and leader—and this vision of herself guided her behaviors and decisions.

Connecting to who you are at your core requires looking at yourself. Getting real with yourself. You need to let go of ideas about what you "should" be doing and instead connect deeply to who you truly are and are not. That's when you make an impact, which then ultimately drives the legacy you create. When working with executives on what they want to be known for, I often hear a deep desire to positively change the trajectory of the lives of others. That's impact!

What do you genuinely want to be known for? At the end of your life, what would you want your eulogy to include? Seriously. I am not trying to be morbid, but we are all going to run our course at some point, so why not be intentional with your contribution to the world and, to guide your choices and behaviors today, begin with the end in mind.

Write Your Eulogy

Adapted from Stephen Covey's *The 7 Habits of Highly Effective People*, this exercise asks you to write your eulogy, how you will be remembered. This may seem a bit heavy, and yet it can be a very powerful exercise in guiding your life choices. It can also bring up a lot of emotion, so choose a time to do this when you have space to visualize the future.

Imagine you are at your own funeral. The space is overflowing with people whose lives you have influenced. Choose four people to speak about you and the difference you made in their lives. They may be close family or friends, work colleagues, or community members. You choose. Use a journal to capture what you would want each person to say that acknowledges who you were for them. Write down all the things that you want to be remembered for. Consider how you would want each to feel when they were with you. Reflect on how you contributed to each of them. How did you change the trajectory of their lives? Write it out as they would speak it: *Nancy was the most courageous person I have had the honor of working with…*

After drafting your eulogy, read through it a couple of times. How does it feel to be acknowledged like this? Do you feel proud? Inspired? Whole? Yes, it may also feel a little presumptuous, but you do want to lead an incredible life and leave a positive mark in the world, don't you?

How do you turn your vision into a reality? Start by determining the daily actions, decisions, and attitudes that align with this vision of yourself. Follow Nancy's practice and identify four or five personal and professional daily practices that support your vision. Then commit to being in practice. Every day.

The rest of your life starts right now.

O2

THE BOSS EFFECT

Choose Your Boss Wisely

Be intentional about the people you choose as your bosses. With each new opportunity, many of us spend countless hours analyzing the job and the company while taking very little time to evaluate the boss we'd be working for. But this is a choice, and taking the time to assess the probable outcomes of your decision can have a lasting impact on your happiness and career trajectory.

So far, I've had fifteen bosses. I believe each was put in my path for a reason, because I had something that needed to be learned. Looking back, I wish I spent less time judging them and more time appreciating what they had to offer. Even the worst bosses taught me some powerful lessons when I looked beneath the surface. These gifts shaped me into the leader I am today.

I think my eighty-year-old self would advise us to find the gifts in everyone we work for. Those we clash with are our most powerful teachers.

Find your freedom in all of it by knowing that you are in the driver's seat; you have control over whom you do and don't work for. When you arrive at your existing job or when you are about to accept a new offer, you are choosing your boss. You would quit your job or decline the offer if you decided against that boss. However, as long as you are showing up, you are choosing this person, so you might as well take advantage of the gifts your boss has to offer. After all, they can have a profound impact on your development and the trajectory of your career.

I created a simple grid that plots knowledge against leadership. Take a closer look at what you might be in store for.

	STRONG FUNCTIONAL EXPERTISE	
STRONG LEADERSHIP EXPERIENCE	Smart Boss	Wise Boss
WEAK LEADERSHIP EXPERIENCE	New Boss	Nice Boss
	WEAK FUNCTIONAL EXPERTISE	

The New Boss: Weak Functional Expertise/ Weak Leadership Experience

New Bosses tend to be over-promoted and placed in leadership positions before they've demonstrated the leadership acumen required for that role. They have an adequate level of intelligence, but they aren't like a Smart Boss. They are less concerned about being the smartest and more focused on the status and power their title brings. However, they often don't realize it is false power. Lacking smarts and leadership, the New Boss tends to feel threatened and lacks the experience required to handle adverse situations, often leaning on Wise Bosses for advice.

I remember my New Boss vividly; he was also my very first boss. My excitement for my very first job out of college was bursting. I was hired to be a personal banker for $25,000 a year. At the time, it felt like so much money. My first big purchase was a new dark purple Saturn. I went to the car dealership with my mom. She made the down payment and I was to be responsible for the monthly payments. I was excited to have a real job and my own car and to finally be out on my own.

Never once did I think about who I was reporting to. All I cared about was getting that job. My boss was the manager of the branch. He was in his late thirties, dressed to the nines every day in a freshly pressed suit, always with a tie (usually a bow tie). He was overly cocky and confident, but I was just starting out and had no reference point for normal behavior. I thought perhaps all bosses at his level were like this.

He offered to take me under his wing and teach me how to be a loan officer. I felt honored and was hungry to learn and advance as quickly as possible. He took me to all of his client meetings, showed me how to write up loan documents, and even started letting me write some of the loans myself with his signature and approval. He was invested in me.

Within months, I was given a raise to $28,000, along with a new desk that was slightly bigger and situated right outside my manager's office. I set a new goal of being a loan officer and felt like I was on the fast track to achieving it.

Then one day I came into work as usual, but something felt off. My boss was not his usual self; he was more reserved and clearly not happy. It was a small bank, the size of an extra-large living room, and it was all one space, so if something was happening, everyone picked up on it.

I saw him go into another manager's office and shut the door. This manager was a tenured loan officer. My boss had a lot of respect for her because of her experience, and, deep down, I think he knew that she was more qualified than he was. I always wondered why *she* wasn't the manager of the branch. She was also nicely dressed in a pressed

I like to ask, "What would my eighty-year-old self say to my younger self?"

suit every day and had a calm confidence about her that I greatly admired. She was respectful of my boss and often responded to his ego and cockiness with humor, deflecting them with a joke or sarcasm that would instantly put him in his place. I would watch her and admire these nuances about her demeanor. I'd make mental notes of her behavior and how she carried herself, as I hoped to someday embody those same characteristics.

My boss was talking angrily and loudly enough that I could hear him through the other manager's office door. He seemed to have an issue with one of the loans I had written. I can't remember exactly what the problem was, but I distinctly remember that he was not happy.

He went from the office of one manager to another, continuing to complain. Then he stormed out and walked across the room to his office on the other side of the branch. I was concerned. I was the golden child who was on the fast track, but something had gone terribly wrong.

One of the managers he had spoken with confirmed that he was unhappy about a loan I had written and suggested I talk to him about it directly so I could learn from my mistakes. I loved the idea of getting direct feedback but was nervous about asking for it.

Later that day, after giving him some time to cool off, I mustered enough courage to walk into my boss's office and ask him for feedback so I could learn and do better next time.

It was as if I had flipped a switch: he got so angry that he puffed up and seemed to grow to double the size. He was a big man in size and stature compared to me. He told me to not tell him what to do, and he proceeded to yell at me at such a volume that everyone in the branch could hear him through the glass walls of his office.

I was embarrassed and humiliated, and no matter how hard I tried, I could not hold back the tears. I stayed sitting in the chair facing his desk, not knowing how to get out of the situation. This was my first job and my instinct was to respect authority. If I left, he would be angrier; if I stayed, he would continue to yell. Then, out of nowhere, came my favorite manager, the one he first talked to that morning. She entered the room, put her hand on my shoulder, and in a very calm but stern voice said to my boss, "That's enough." She told me to leave and remained with him for a few more minutes, until he eventually calmed down.

When I interviewed for the job, he seemed like such a great guy. On the outside, he was charismatic with customers and other employees of the bank; however, his insecurities hovered just beneath the surface.

Roles under a New Boss can feel exciting at the onset but can quickly turn on you the minute the insecurities set in. The beauty of a New Boss is they are typically in the early stages of their career and hopefully will seek out ways to improve over time.

The Smart Boss: Strong Functional Expertise/ Weak Leadership Experience

Smart Bosses exist in most organizations. They work very hard to be the smartest person in the room at all times, often trumping every idea and always having the last word. Smart Bosses can be the most abrasive type, yet they often don't realize they come across this way.

One particular Smart Boss stands out for me. At the time, I felt so lucky to have finally found a manager who really valued me. But the red flags surfaced shortly thereafter. I quickly realized that behind closed doors, he had nothing nice to say about anyone in the organization. He described my predecessor as "a good riddance" and the people who remained as "very junior."

Putting down others made him feel smart and powerful. At least once a week, he would declare that he believed he was "the smartest person in the company" and that "no one else knows the work and the industry like I do."

He was handsome and always well dressed and put together. He was short in stature, in good physical shape, and in his mid-thirties. And while he appeared to have it all, for some reason, he felt the need to push people around to get his way. He made it known that if anyone crossed him, there would be repercussions. People were scared of him so they would do as he said, which ultimately gave him no reason to stop. He was driven by false power, intimidating people by way of his title instead of encouraging them through influence.

At the end of the day, he was, in fact, very smart. However, he didn't know everything, nor did I find him to be the smartest person in the company. He knew what he knew, and he knew it well. He taught me how to dissect a failing business and rebuild it from the ground up, down to every last detail. He was obsessed with numbers and analytics to track and measure our success.

I learned how to manage a business at a level of granularity I never thought possible. I was micromanaged on a daily basis and rarely had space to think outside the box. I also learned vehemently how to *not* lead teams. Seeing the amount of damage a Smart Boss can do on a team of passionate, talented individuals over a few short months inspired me to define my leadership in a different way.

Learning from a Smart Boss can be extremely painful at times, yet it can also be a great learning experience. I can say this was true for me on many levels. However, it is important to take your learning and run, as a Smart Boss will stifle you and prevent you from achieving your full potential.

The Nice Boss: Weak Functional Expertise/ Strong Leadership Experience

Nice Bosses are the best because they are, well, so nice. It feels good to work for them as they typically have extreme

"

Had I chosen a
Wise Boss in each of
my roles, and never
settled for anything
less, it's possible that
my career could have
gone further, faster.

"

wisdom, life experience, and perspective to offer. However, because they have been in leadership positions for a very long time, they are often far removed from the work to the point where they have lost touch with the details of it.

I have fond memories of my favorite Nice Boss. He was nearing retirement, and by that point, he was in a blissful state, having held several senior leadership roles. He served the company we worked for as a figurehead of sorts, a big hire from a well-known brand, and provided wonderful leadership, advice, and mentorship.

But he was hired as the head of marketing without strong experience in digital strategy, in an era where everything was digital in nature. For several years, our team spent the majority of the time explaining to and teaching him the importance of our work and why it was vital. This posed a serious problem because he didn't have the knowledge to represent our work or back up our strategic investments.

While it can become comfortable working under a Nice Boss, the bottom line is to enjoy them for their wisdom and experience—but don't stay too long. It is too easy to become stagnant under the leadership of a Nice Boss.

The Wise Boss: Strong Functional Expertise/ Strong Leadership Experience

Wise Bosses are calm, confident, and egoless. They have done the work themselves, earned their stripes, and grown into their leadership from the ground up. They have been guided and coached by the best and seek out a massive amount of leadership training wherever they can find it.

They are constantly learning and view feedback as a gift, welcoming it from every level of the organization. They view not only superiors as their coaches but also those who are subordinate to them. They lean into young talent and believe it is their role to coach and develop the next generation to be bigger, better, faster, and stronger than they were.

They are young at heart and have been around the block with decades of experience that gives them the wisdom to see the big picture and put even the greatest of challenges in perspective.

They are vulnerable, compassionate, and generous, and they always make time for you.

Of the fifteen managers I've had, only two of them were Wise Bosses.

I've learned from every single manager I've had: the Smart ones, the New ones, the Nice ones, and the Wise ones. Each has offered me tremendous gifts that I have taken to heart.

Remember that you always have a choice, so choose wisely.

Get Coached to Work Freely

I invite you to consider two things: choosing your boss and being the boss people choose.

Choosing Your Boss

Research suggests that people quit their bosses, not their companies. However, many people do not adequately take the time to "hire" their bosses. We are often so excited at the possibility of a new job or about the organization that either we don't inquire about who our potential leader is or we ignore the indicators. It's not unlike when we first meet a potential romantic partner. We want to experience them as "perfect," and we dismiss the potential misalignments. This is not to say that they (or your potential bosses) are broken. But your core values or expectations may not be aligned.

Our goal here is that you learn to discern the qualities in a boss that are important to you, so that you can legitimately be in a position to choose who you work for.

Before you start your next dialogue with a potential organization and/or leader, try the following exercise. The Power of Knowing What You Want, developed by my mentor and Lightyear Leadership founder Susanne Conrad (www.lightyear.co), is a simple, meaningful way to articulate and clarify what you desire—generally, in your life, or more specifically, in a boss. In the words of Susanne, "It is all too common that people focus on what they don't want in their lives instead of getting clear about what they do want. It is essential to create this clarity before writing a vision and goals. By completing the circle exercise, you can begin to clarify what it is you do want in the future." Consider using this exercise any time you wish to gain clarity in your life. A downloadable pdf of The Power of Knowing What You Want is available at www.workfreely.co.

STEP 1: Draw a circle on a piece of paper, the circle taking up 75 percent of the page.

STEP 2: Inside the circle, clearly and explicitly state everything you want in a boss. This may include qualities, skills, and behaviors, and it may also include how you want to feel when you work with this leader. This will be very personal to you. Some examples are "thought partner," "champion," "confident," "humble," "clear decision maker," and "I feel empowered, seen, understood, and capable."

STEP 3: Add color. Highlight or circle your non-negotiables—those qualities that you cannot live without—in one color and your "nice-to-haves" in a different color.

STEP 4: Outside the circle, write anything you don't want in a boss, creating a clear boundary. It is important to take time to get clear on what you want and do not want. Again,

"THERE ARE ONLY
TWO WAYS TO
INFLUENCE HUMAN
BEHAVIOR: YOU CAN
MANIPULATE IT OR
YOU CAN INSPIRE IT."

SIMON SINEK

this will be very personal, and some examples include "controlling," "abusive," and "not confident."

Why take the time to do this exercise? I am a firm believer of the law of attraction, meaning that we get what we focus on, whether we want it or not. So why did I ask you to look at what you don't want and put those things outside the circle? Great question! It's important to know what you don't want so that you can very clearly choose what you do want.

Once you know what you do and don't want, you may interview your potential boss and be willing to make a choice based on their responses.

Possible questions to ask your potential boss include the following:

- Who are you as a leader?
- What are your current development goals as a leader?
- What strengthens/energizes you as a leader? What weakens/exhausts you?
- How do you deal with challenge/adversity/change?
- When are you at your best?
- When are you at your worst?
- What would you count on me for?
- What could I count on you for?
- How would others describe you as a leader?

- What significant failure have you experienced? What did you learn from it?
- What has been the toughest yet most helpful feedback you've ever received?
- What would happen if I disagreed with you?
- Why would I want you as a boss?
- Why would I *not* want you as a boss?
- What can I learn from you?
- What do you want to learn from me?
- To what degree will I be able to influence change?
- How much autonomy will I have? (Note: consider how much autonomy you want!)
- What will my decision-making authority be?

Any of the four kinds of bosses that Nancy described have something to offer, depending on what you want at a particular time in your career. What are the conditions in which you will thrive now? What are your goals and objectives? And what type of boss will support you in achieving that?

Once you've asked the questions and received the answers: What happens if your potential boss responds in a way that does not align with what you need?

Let's assume you take a job with this boss. A year passes. The "honeymoon phase" is over. Connect with your future self and ask what you need to know. What has it been like working in this organization, for this boss? What's working? What's not? What does your future self appreciate? And regret? Spend time with your future self, who has the answers. Only you know what is right for you.

Being the Boss People Choose

This is a great time to review your work on legacy from chapter 1. Are you living that vision of how you want to be remembered? Where would people currently place you in the four quadrants? Is their experience of you aligned with your vision of yourself?

Consider going through the questions above with your direct reports and really listen to what your people tell you. Replace "boss" with "colleagues" if you currently do not have direct reports and are considering how you want your colleagues to experience you. Engaging in this type of learning dialogue is a powerful example of Wise Boss behavior and will not only strengthen the trust your people have in you but also provide you with valuable gifts of insight on your leadership journey, which never truly ends.

03
BREADWINNER

Master Your Fear

Fear of the unknown often prevents us from moving boldly forward and making decisions that serve us. *I might not get that promotion... I might not make enough money... I'll be seen as a quitter... My bonus is on the line...* By letting these thoughts take over, we give up the life we want to live. But when we find the confidence to master our fears, we access new levels of freedom in our choices.

At twenty-five, I was hired to be a full-blown officer at a local bank in Seattle. My new manager's name was Dave. Turns out, he was a Wise Boss. I had chosen well.

He was a smart, confident family man. I guessed he was about ten years older than me. He was happily married with two small children. Dave was a coach and a mentor through and through. He spent months teaching me everything I needed to know to be a successful lender. He pushed and held me accountable but was always there to pick me up and provide coaching if I made a mistake.

Dave was the epitome of a servant-leader. He always put his people first, taking a back seat, and leading from behind. He knew that his success was the success of his team. When his team won, he won. Every day he came to work to teach, educate, and develop people. And he was always genuinely happy to see people thrive.

Being a loan officer was such a rush that it was almost addicting; the more you worked, the more money you made. It was also one of the scariest jobs I ever had, given it was 100 percent commission-based. If I didn't close loans, I didn't make money.

Shortly after starting the job, I married Sean. I met Sean on the soccer field. We were both competitive soccer players, playing on Division 1 coed soccer teams after university.

We met one night at a game where he was the captain of the opposing team. I vividly recall him walking over to our huddle before the game. He exuded a calm confidence that I found incredibly attractive.

He was a defender and I was a forward, so naturally throughout the game we kept running into each other. He was happy, chatty, confident, and funny.

I had a boyfriend at the time, but I knew I was in a relationship that was not going to last. Sean asked me out a couple of times, but I declined given the circumstances. He graciously told me to give him a call when I was single. Nine months later, I was single and so I called. Luckily, he was still single too.

Within two months, we bought a car together. A few months later, we bought a house. One month after that, we adopted a puppy. And two months later, we were engaged. We were married the following year and within nine months, I gave birth to a beautiful baby girl.

Sean and I decided that I would be the one to work and he would stay home. I lived to work and had big career aspirations, so it was a natural decision. At twenty-seven years old, I had a husband, a baby, and a German shepherd puppy, and I was the breadwinner of the family. This was a huge responsibility and one that I did not take lightly.

I worked my loan-officer job until the moment I went into labor. And within three days, I was back to work.

I had a traumatic delivery that ended in a C-section. I remember leaving the house to go to work and looking at Sean lying on the couch with this tiny little human being in his arms, an image that will forever be ingrained in my mind. When I tell the story now, fifteen years later, the memory is just as vivid as it was the day I walked out the door.

As I reflect on this moment, it feels ridiculous that I would go back to work so soon after having a baby and major surgery. When I went back to work, I was flooded with guilt for leaving my baby so soon, only breastfeeding for a few days before turning the bottle over to my husband to provide sustenance for her. But at the time, it felt necessary, as if I had no choice. I needed to make money, to support the family, and I was worried I would fall behind in my career progress if I took any time off. I didn't want any special treatment for being a woman or a mom, nor did I want to be faulted for it. I wanted to be known for doing great work, exceeding expectations, and hitting my bonuses just like anyone else in the office.

But my motivation was driven by fear—fear of not making enough money to support the family and fear of not advancing my career at the rate of my peers. The immense pressure driven by the fear of falling behind came from no one other than myself. This ultimately held me back from making meaningful life decisions at a critical moment. If I could go back in time, I would take every last second I could get at home with my babies. No one will ever remember the sacrifice I made, but I always will.

Get Coached to Work Freely

I appreciate Nancy's vulnerability in sharing what she was going through as a new mother and her perception that going back to work was the only choice. I too know

"WHAT'S THE GREATER
RISK? LETTING GO
OF WHAT PEOPLE
THINK—OR LETTING
GO OF HOW I FEEL,
WHAT I BELIEVE, AND
WHO I AM?"

BRENÉ BROWN

what it is like to make decisions out of fear. In 2005, I was diagnosed with breast cancer. The very first thought that entered my mind when I heard the diagnosis was: "How am I going to pay my mortgage?" I was single at the time and, six months earlier, had just purchased my first home. Anxiety about my finances drove me to continue working full-time through months of surgeries, chemotherapy, and radiation, leading to exhaustion and depression by the end of my treatment. At the time, I saw it as choosing to be strong and resilient. But it wasn't a choice at all, because I was being driven by fear, attempting to avoid the discomfort of admitting that I might need financial support or that I didn't have it all together.

Here is the thing: there is absolutely no freedom in fear. Zero. And when we believe that there is only one option, that isn't a choice at all. To be able to choose, you must see at least two options as viable.

Choice uses the prefrontal cortex, the part of our brain that is responsible for analyzing, considering, and making rational decisions. It's the executive part of our brain that allows us to respond instead of reacting. When responding from that place, we ask, *What is most important? What is needed here? What is possible?* When we operate out of fear, we say, *How do I avoid failing? Or being hurt? Or being rejected?* Chris Argyris refers to these as "defensive habits." This way of experiencing the world can start to control you.

We all have an inner critic—I call it a saboteur—that speaks in "shoulds" and "can'ts." You shouldn't ask for what you want. You can't take a risk. You shouldn't rock the boat. You can't let them know you're scared. The purpose of the saboteur is to protect you from the discomfort of failing, being rejected, admitting you were wrong, asking for help, or otherwise being vulnerable. It originates from the part of the brain called the amygdala, and it serves a purpose when you are in imminent danger of being hit by a bus and you react by jumping out of the way. Unfortunately, it doesn't typically serve you well when it hijacks your otherwise great ability to rationalize, discern, and make sound choices. That might look like going back to work three days after giving birth over fear of falling behind, even though family and health are extremely important. It might look like avoiding a candid, crucial conversation with a direct report or your boss that could elevate the relationship and/or results, for fear of how it might go.

Opportunities emerge when we have the courage to say no to those things that we don't want and make space for what we do truly want. Try this on a blank piece of paper:

STEP 1: In which area(s) of your life is "should" present? Fill in the blank: I should be _____.

STEP 2: Replace "should" with "want to" or "get to." I want to _____. I get to _____.

At any given moment, we
are either responding out of
choice or acting out of fear.
When responding out of
choice, we are connected
to what we most cherish,
what is most important.

STEP 3: Reflect on how that feels. Is this "should" what you really want?

Fear is natural. It helps us pay attention. However, making fear-based decisions usually just means you're paying more attention to what you don't want. To shift your relationship with fear, get to know it better. Where is it running your life? What are you afraid of?

Identify one career- or life-related fear and begin to master it by writing down your answers to the following:

- What do you really want?
- What first step can you make toward what you want?
- Who else do you need to include in this conversation to support you and to be a sounding board?
- Do you need to make a decision about it right now?

Fear likely will not be conquered in one pass through this exercise. But asking yourself these questions repeatedly will help you develop your critical thinking and executive decision-making muscles. Be real with yourself and listen deeply to your answers. It may be uncomfortable at first, and you may be tempted to avoid such reflection. Stick with it! Just like working out, the more you do it, the easier it will get. What may be tiring now will soon energize you as you connect to what is truly most in service of your life.

O4

THE NEW NORMAL

Do Life Your Way, Not the "Done" Way

There will always be advocates of your decisions in
life—and there will always be skeptics. With each new generation, cultural norms change, but only because someone
had the courage to challenge the status quo and be at the
vanguard until the rest of the world caught up. Be embold-
ened to do life your way, not the way others have done it
before or the way they want you to do it now.

The decision for Sean to stay at home was a pretty
easy one, but implementing the plan was another story.
This was 2003, and the "stay-at-home dad" concept was
not a normal thing yet. People always assumed that Sean
would work and I would stay home. Whenever I told others about what we were doing, I was met with glazed looks
and awkward responses.

Sean liked the term "house husband" and would gladly inform people of his occupation if ever asked. And without fail, he would smile and say, "I'm the luckiest guy I know." I would get a chuckle out of that statement every time he said it.

Sean established his own unique stay-at-home-dad "uniform," as he called it, which he wore every day. A button-down checkered shirt, cargo shorts, runners, a binky clipped to the left pocket of his shirt, and a camouflaged diaper bag backpack. He drove a big black truck large enough to haul a gaggle of kids and our German shepherd.

In the beginning, the mommies left him out of the groups because it was not the norm for a guy to hang out with the women as they talked about delivery complications, painful breastfeeding, and recovery after birth. But over time he became a rock star with all the moms. They were his friends. They'd meet up on the playground, at school functions, at field trips, and at playdates. He was one of those parents who knew almost everyone at the school—it was his superpower. He could identify and remember parents by the type of car they drove. And before sending one of our kids on a playdate with a kid whose parents he didn't know, Sean would google them and make sure they weren't a child molester or a convicted felon. He kept a cheat sheet in the notes section of his phone to help him remember everyone.

I loved that he was so connected.

It always gave me a sense of pride to know that we were doing it our way and making it work.

I would attempt to share the household duties, but for the most part Sean handled everything from doing the laundry, cooking meals, gardening, and doing most of the cleaning. This way, I could focus on spending time with him and the kids when I was home. We call him the "COO" of the household.

Every once in a while, I would try to help out with other things, like the grocery shopping. However, because I rarely set foot in a grocery store, I felt extremely out of place and struggled to find things. It was like foreign territory. One day, Sean sent me to get some fabric softener, and I stood in the laundry aisle for ten minutes scanning the shelves, until I realized I had no idea what fabric softener was. Was it a liquid? Or maybe paper? Did it come in a box or a bottle? Was it soap or something else? Was it used in the dryer or the washer? I literally had no idea because I never did the laundry. I finally left empty-handed, and I still have no idea what fabric softener is, although it sounds very nice.

I managed the finances and paid the bills and we had joint checking accounts. My money was his money. He was the reason I was able to have a thriving career, and I was the reason he was able to stay home and raise our kids. We viewed it as shared success.

With only one household income, we lived on a very tight budget. I often envied the families that had two working parents. How nice it must have been to have two paychecks. We could have really used the extra money when we were starting out. I specifically remember one day we had nothing in our bank account and we needed gas for the car, so we emptied out the kids' piggy banks and scraped up just enough for us to buy gas to last for the rest of the week. For us, the financial sacrifice was worth having one parent home with our kids. We didn't quite understand the impact of our unusual decision and how it was shaping them, until one particular day.

My daughter was seven, and she had a boy over for a playdate. They decided to play house. He put on a coat, grabbed his briefcase, and said, "Honey, I'm going to work."

My daughter, dumbfounded, looked sternly at the boy and said, "No, silly, the *mom* goes to work and the *dad* stays home with the kids."

I will never forget that moment. It signified a milestone in our life, where I felt like we were breaking new ground, raising curious and open-minded children, and crushing gender roles in the household.

Now, as my babies are becoming teenagers, I am proud of the individuals they've become and feel the sacrifice and struggle were well worth it. Over the last fifteen years, the concept of the stay-at-home dad has become more commonly understood and accepted. It has even started to take on a cool factor, where men who stay home are seen as confident, capable, and well-rounded. And women who work feel empowered, strong, and supported.

I urged Sean to start a blog back in the day, but he was never into it. He cared about the real, authentic relationships he had with his friends and did not have an interest in being recognized on a bigger platform. Although he never hit the grand stage, I believe he's played a major role in paving the way for new dads to embrace the role of the house husband and begin to discover their superpowers.

Get Coached to Work Freely

I grew up in a very "traditional" family, where my dad worked, my mom stayed at home, and at an early age my two sisters and I were given dolls. As we progressed through high school, we were presented with some pretty limited options for our postsecondary journeys: teaching, nursing, business, or general arts. Although we as a society—in North America at least—are now busting through these limiting views, and I have girlfriends who are firefighters, surgeons, and CEOs and guy friends who are hairstylists, nurses, and designers, it takes courage to forge the path less traveled, to create freedom in your big life choices, as did Nancy and Sean.

Their whole situation shouts freedom. What allowed them to bust through societal norms, what was expected and accepted?

They were very clear on the life they wanted to create for their family. They had done the work of determining what they wanted and what they did not want. (The Power of Knowing What You Want from chapter 2 is a great tool for determining this.) Their roles reflected their unique strengths and passions. And in living into those roles, they helped their children learn that anything is possible.

Their decision was led by their core values. Nancy shares how she connected to her values in chapter 8. Core values guide your choices. They let people know what you stand for. They remind you of what you stand for.

Core values ideally determine your priorities, and, deep down, they're probably the measures you use to tell if your life is turning out the way you want it to. When you behave in a way and do things that match your values, life is usually good—you're content. But when you do things that don't align with your values, life feels . . . off. This can be a real source of unhappiness.

Life can be much easier when you acknowledge your values, making decisions and plans that honor them. If you value family, but you work sixty-plus-hour weeks, will you feel internal stress and conflict? And if you don't value competition, but you work in a highly competitive sales environment, are you likely to be satisfied with your job?

When you know your own values, you can use them to make decisions about how to live, and you can answer questions like these:

- What is my ideal job/role?
- How does this promotion fit with my vision and my values?
- What will enable me to live and work freely?
- Where am I compromising myself and what is most important?
- Should I follow tradition or travel down a new path?

Take the time to understand the real priorities in your life, and you'll be able to determine the best direction for you and your goals.

Values are usually fairly stable, yet they don't have strict limits or boundaries. Also, as you move through life, your values may change. For example, when you start your career, success—measured by money and status—might be a top priority. But after you have a family, work-life balance may be what you value most.

Determining Your Values

As you connect more deeply with what's really true for you, your definition of success may change. This is why staying in touch with your values is a lifelong practice. Revisit the following exercise regularly, especially if you start to feel unbalanced and you can't quite figure out why. The following exercise can be used to help you identify your core values, as well as to periodically check in with what is true and important for you throughout your life and career. I recommend coming back to this at key milestones and choice points in your life.

STEP 1: Identify the times when you were happiest. Find examples from both your career and your personal life. This will ensure some balance in your answers. For each example, answer the following:

- What were you doing?
- Were you with other people? Who?
- What other factors contributed to your happiness?

STEP 2: Identify the times when you were proudest. Use examples from your career and personal life. For each example, answer the following:

- Why were you proud?
- Did other people share your pride? Who?
- What other factors contributed to your feelings of pride?

STEP 3: Identify the times when you were most fulfilled and satisfied. Again, use both work and personal examples and answer the following:

- What need or desire was fulfilled?
- How and why did the experience give your life meaning?
- What other factors contributed to your feelings of fulfillment?

STEP 4: Determine your top values, based on your experiences of happiness, pride, and fulfillment. Why is each experience truly important and memorable?

Use the following list of common personal values to help you get started. The list below is a small sample, so please add any words you feel are missing but that apply to your examples, or visit www.workfreely.co for a fuller list. As you work through this exercise, you may find that some of your values naturally combine. For instance, if you value philanthropy, community, and generosity, you might say that service to others is one of your top values. Aim for a list of about ten top values.

Accountability	Growth
Ambition	Humility
Being the best	Intellectual status
Challenge	Justice
Competitiveness	Loyalty
Curiosity	Originality
Dynamism	Reliability
Elegance	Resourcefulness
Excitement	Service
Faith	Shrewdness
Fitness	Simplicity
Freedom	Teamwork
Fun	Timeliness
Generosity	Vitality

STEP 5: Prioritize your values. In no particular order, write down your top ten values. Compare the first two items on the list and ask yourself, *If I could satisfy only one of these, which would I choose?* (It might help to visualize a situation in which you would have to make that choice. For example, if you compare the values of service and stability, imagine that you must decide whether to sell your house and move to another country to do valuable foreign aid work or keep your house and volunteer to do charity work closer to home.) Keep working through the list until you have compared all the values and the list is in the correct order.

Step 5 is probably the most difficult because it requires that you look deep inside yourself. It's also the most important step because, when making a decision, you often have to choose between solutions that satisfy different values. This is when you must know which value is more important to you.

STEP 6: Reaffirm your values. Review your top-priority values and make sure they fit with your vision for your life. Do these values make you feel good about yourself? Are you proud of your top three values? Would you be proud to tell people you respect and admire about your values? Do these values represent things you support, even if your choice isn't popular and it puts you in the minority?

"YOU HAVE YOUR WAY.

I HAVE MY WAY. AS

FOR THE RIGHT WAY,

THE CORRECT WAY,

AND THE ONLY WAY,

IT DOES NOT EXIST."

FRIEDRICH NIETZSCHE

When you consider your values in decision making, you keep your sense of integrity and approach decisions with confidence and clarity. You also know that your choice is best for your current and future happiness. Making value-based decisions may not always be easy. However, making a choice that you know is right is a lot less difficult in the long run.

Wheel of Life

When you're making choices that align with your values, you feel energized. Confident. Authentic. And you also know when you are not honoring your values. You may feel frustrated. Out of flow. Like something is missing.

Staying true to what is most important for you takes courage at times. I recommend doing a quarterly check-in using the Wheel of Life.

STEP 1: Draw a pie chart that includes a slice for each realm of your life. (See an example on the next page. You may find that some of your categories are different, but you can use these as a guide.)

STEP 2: For each realm, rate how fulfilled you are in each realm on a scale of 1 to 10. As in the illustration, you might also use color or shading to indicate the level of each category.

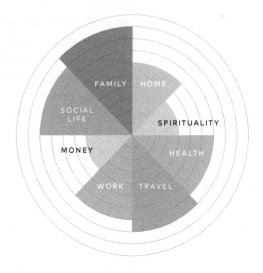

How fulfilled are you currently in each of your realms? How fulfilled do you want to be? This may seem like a strange question and you may be thinking, *Of course I want to be a 10 in everything.* Consider that certain areas of life take priority over others at different times. When starting a new job, you may be a 10 in the realm of career. You're feeling fulfilled, excited by the possibilities, energized by the learning. When nearing retirement or a six-month sabbatical to go traveling, your career may not be at a "fulfillment high," and being at a 6 could be exactly what you want. There is no right or wrong way to look at this; just be honest about what makes you feel your best.

Have a Word with Yourself

You know when you are not connected to your best self, when things are off. You feel frustrated or unsatisfied. Curiosity and compassion are hijacked by judgment and impatience. Your joy tank is running on empty. This is usually an indication that you are out of balance in one or more areas of your life that are really important for you. I know I'm out of balance when I'm eating takeout a lot. One of the ways I express my core values of vitality and creativity is to take the time to design yummy meal plans for my husband and me, then make those meals with fresh, colorful ingredients as I drink my homemade kombucha. When I don't make the time for this ritual, and I find myself bringing takeout home for dinner more than once a week, I feel out of sorts. I get frustrated. It's a sign that I'm taking on too much and not making space for me, my health, and my relationship. Of course, this is going to happen periodically, but if it becomes the norm, I need to have a word with myself and be honest about what I say yes to and what I say no to.

Have a word with yourself. What adjustments do you need to make to get back in integrity with a life that works for you?

DEFINE
YOUR
LEADERSHIP

05
ONE MILLION LIKES

Make Your Role Obsolete

Peak performers often feel on the verge of being fired. Others see them as extremely competent and capable, but because they have such high standards for themselves, they constantly feel they could be doing more, faster, better, stronger. They often take on more work and do the job of ten people. There *can* be freedom in a job well done, but strong leaders know that doing a good job is often about letting go and holding space for others to thrive.

In the first ten years of my career, I pushed as hard as I could, constantly comparing myself to others, always trying to prove I was worthy. I saw my peers as competition and judged those who were in positions I felt I deserved. My view was that you only have one shot in your lifetime to get to the top, and I intended to make the most of it. And yet, I kept getting overlooked. Things weren't progressing fast enough. The world was moving so quickly while my advancement felt like it was moving at a snail's pace.

I couldn't understand why this was happening when I was working so hard, putting in a massive number of hours, and delivering on my responsibilities. I didn't realize at the time that, although I was delivering on the *functional* requirements of my job, my *leadership* was severely lacking. And because of this, the good work I did was being overshadowed by who I was being and how I showed up. I constantly got in the way of myself—pulled into the office gossip, dragged down by daily frustrations, and consumed by reorgs, reporting structures, and titles.

"Leadership" is a grossly overused term. I knew I needed more of it, but I didn't know what it really meant or how to get it. Then I was hired to join lululemon. It was not only an athletic apparel company; it was a brand on a mission to develop leaders in the world. I used to believe the harder I pushed, the further I would get. But I quickly learned that when I softened, stepped back, let go, and focused inward on who I was being for others, good things started to happen.

My drive, raw determination, and tenacity were the qualities that got me to this point, but they also would cause me to fail and hit a ceiling if I continued down this path. To access the next level of leadership that would propel

Leadership means building a team that delivers in your presence yet thrives in your absence.

me forward, I needed to take a fundamentally different approach.

And so I decided to make my role obsolete.

I loved my job and I felt like I had a long career and runway ahead of me at lululemon. I wasn't planning to go anywhere. However, I knew that if I approached each day with the intention of making my role obsolete, I would become more of a teacher. I'd be more focused on educating and developing capable teams and less focused on helping and advancing my own career. This process required a level of vulnerability that made me feel uncomfortable.

I made it a ritual to remind myself of this every day before I went in to work.

It was like flexing a muscle until it became a habit. At the time, I was a Smart Boss, so it took a lot for me to trust others to do the job as well as or better than I could. I discovered there was enormous power in saying "I trust you." It became part of my vocabulary. Whenever I would say it, people would light up and take on a greater sense of responsibility and pride in their work.

I vividly remember one circumstance at lululemon, about three years in, where I named one of the brand managers as my proxy. Her name was Lesia Dallimore. Lesia is one of the most hilarious and talented human beings I have ever worked with. She is quick-witted and has a self-deprecating style of humor that makes her real, human, and approachable. Inside the company, she was a powerful force when it came to brand and product. She was a smart, strategic entrepreneur who found ways to get things done with quality on a shoestring budget. An email marketer by trade, she quickly grew to be a director in the company. She was an emotionally intelligent leader that many people were drawn to because she cared deeply about every individual—her peers and her managers. She was one of the few who worked well with everyone up, down, and across the organization.

I was headed down to Tacoma, Washington, to visit our kids' great-grandmother. It was an important trip that we thought might be our last before she passed away. I knew I could not be online all week so I left Lesia in charge.

Within twenty-four hours, I got a text from her that said, "Hey Nancy, we decided to make a video. We need you to approve it so we can post it on YouTube today. We have a goal of getting to one million likes in a week." Instead of looking at the video, I trusted her to approve it herself and keep running. She and the team spent three dollars on a carton of almond milk, produced the video with three people, and hit one million likes in less than a week. It was pure gold.

When I returned from my trip, the floor was buzzing with excitement and an entrepreneurial energy spurred on by a great idea executed with passion and heart. This

The real issue was not whether they were talented enough to do the work. The real issue was my confidence in letting go and realizing they could do the work ten times better.

happened over and over again. I was constantly impressed with what people were capable of when they were trusted and given the space to create. It required getting out of my own head, being generous instead of protective, developing and trusting others, and then letting go. We called this "the work of the work."

Get Coached to Work Freely

What do you experience when you consider working to make your role obsolete? Excitement? Determination? Skepticism? Doubt? If you are less than keen about it, you are not alone. Most leaders do not strive to work themselves out of a job. After all, it could mean giving up something that you love, that fulfills you, that challenges you. And if you give away your responsibilities to your team, then what will you do?

But leaders who strive to make themselves obsolete don't see it as losing something; they see it as gaining something: space. Space to mentor, coach, and delegate. By developing your people to take on your responsibilities, you create space for new opportunities, bigger problems to tackle, higher-stakes games to play, or deeper, more meaningful connection to what is most important to you. It gives you space to live into your legacy in bigger and more impactful ways.

This mind-set takes confidence and sometimes courage. It takes being deeply connected to your legacy and seeing movement as a necessary step in fulfilling it.

It relies on you hiring people who are smarter, brighter, and different than you, and allowing them to shine. It sometimes depends on you giving up the driver's seat and letting go of having to do things your way. It means getting out of the way of your people.

This is much easier if you are clear on what you are gaining. What is your motivation? For Nancy, it was the deep satisfaction of developing an exceptional team of leaders for the world—an expression of her purpose. For some, it is about gaining the time to take on their next big goals. For others, it is the space to start thinking about what those next big goals might be.

What will you gain from making your role obsolete?

To get clearer on your answer, create a "Work toward Obsolescence" quadrant and fill it out, either in a journal or in a printable version you can download from www.workfreely.co.

"BEING THE LEADER MEANS YOU HOLD THE HIGHEST RANK, EITHER BY EARNING IT, GOOD FORTUNE, OR NAVIGATING INTERNAL POLITICS. LEADING, HOWEVER, MEANS THAT OTHERS WILLINGLY FOLLOW YOU— NOT BECAUSE THEY HAVE TO, NOT BECAUSE THEY ARE PAID TO, BUT BECAUSE THEY WANT TO."

SIMON SINEK

Work toward Obsolescence Quadrant

Work toward Obsolescence What I may gain:	Work toward Obsolescence What it might cost me:
Continue Current Way of Leading What I may gain:	Continue Current Way of Leading What it might cost me:

This is not intended to be a simplistic cost/benefit analysis; rather, it's a way for you to identify and then explore your current perceptions, assumptions, and desires. Take time to consider each quadrant for your life beyond your work. What stands out for you? What do you see as important? How do your values show up? Where does fear creep in? What assumptions do you need to check out?

Connect with what you do and don't want as a leader, and answer these questions:

- What do I need to start doing?
- What do I need to stop doing?
- Who do I need to start being?
- Who do I need to stop being?

What will you commit to today? This week? Next week? Next month? How will you hold yourself accountable? How will you acknowledge your progress?

06

DAILY MANTRA

Flex New Leadership Muscles

Sometimes work just happens. It's easy to fall into a rut of walking into meetings, giving presentations, and delivering performance reviews without really thinking about them. Sometimes things go well. But sometimes they don't, and you have to course-correct after the fact. Leadership commitments can serve as a daily mantra and anchor during challenging times.

Leadership is a never-ending journey. Every day brings new challenges, some bigger than others. In the corporate roles I've held, there were always balls up in the air and a constant barrage of judgments and criticisms that evoked strong emotions. These led me to make rash decisions, say things I would regret, or write emails I could not retract. Success, in my mind, was learning how to move through these situations with grace and professionalism.

One meeting in particular challenged me in more ways than one. It was scheduled by the CEO at the last minute. There were no notes in advance, just the subject "Meeting with the CEO."

A dozen people were invited, mostly directors and above, with one manager sitting in as a proxy for her director.

The CEO had been out for two months straight, but on this particular Friday, he unexpectedly arrived in the office and held the meeting in a room called "The Bunker." It was dark, without windows, located at the end of a long hallway in the back corner of the office. There were other, more pleasant rooms available, with more space and light, but instead he chose The Bunker.

When I arrived, I chose the seat next to him. His energy was angry. My natural inclination was to stay close to him. When people are angry or irrationally emotional, I become unusually calm; it's like a natural survival instinct.

Most of the attendees were my direct reports. Once we had gathered, he asked each person to share what they felt was working and not working. He had a history of asking people for their thoughts and then belittling them in front of their peers, stating all the reasons why they were wrong. This time was no different.

The marketing director went first and then each person followed, one by one. I was proud of my team as they brought up how leadership was falling short, how the

66

When women stand up
for themselves, they are
called out and viewed as
emotional and part of the
problem. When men do the
same thing, their behavior
is viewed as passionate
and part of the solution.

99

change in strategic priorities was influencing productivity and quality of work, and how the directives were contributing to burnout and low morale.

The CEO took notes as each person shared, and when everyone was done, as expected, he went around the room and explained to each person how they were wrong. He spoke as if no one understood the basics of business. Everyone sat there and took the hurtful, demeaning, degrading insults. To make it worse, the CEO made personal, disrespectful, and sarcastic comments to all individuals in the room, as if their work was a joke.

During this tirade, his anger escalated. He yelled, swore, and came across as manic, telling everyone their number-one job was to "make me look good." I tried to interject a couple of times, but he directed me to "sit down and stop being so defensive of people."

After the meeting, he pulled me aside and reminded me, again, that my job was to make him look good. I said very little because I was conflicted about whether to push back or let it go. I was scared that if I challenged him, he would get even angrier. I had lost my footing and was disappointed in myself in that moment.

I needed a way of managing through scenarios like this without losing myself. As I replayed the meeting in my mind, I realized I needed better tools in my back pocket to counteract the CEO's behavior, so I came up with a method that would help see me through such challenging scenarios in the future.

HIS REACTION	MY COMMITMENT
Fear	Courage
Hate	Compassion
Anger	Calm
Doubt	Confidence
Defensiveness	Curiosity

It's easy to be great when things are going well, but the moments when you are tested determine your character and show your true colors. These five commitments (courage, compassion, calm, confidence, and curiosity, or the 5 Cs, as I like to call them) have helped me counteract emotionally charged people, harsh judgments, personal criticism, and those who believe they have all the answers. These commitments forced me to be more positive and productive in the moment, and they became a mantra of sorts.

"WHAT IS THE DIFFERENCE BETWEEN REACTING AND RESPONDING? ABOUT TEN SECONDS."

UNKNOWN

Everyone has unique emotions that require a unique set of commitments. My rule of thumb is that you choose three to five commitments that you can easily remember.

If I had this tool in my back pocket that day in The Bunker, I would have been able to handle things more powerfully in the moment. I know that I am the best version of myself when I'm operating with all 5 Cs.

Get Coached to Work Freely

I would like to introduce a sixth C. Choice. We have talked about it a lot throughout the book and this is what each of Nancy's 5 Cs is grounded in. You react out of anger. You choose to be compassionate (to self or to others). You react with defensiveness. You choose to be curious. And so on. This leads to a seventh C. Consciousness.

It takes consciousness to remain connected to your best self—courageous, compassionate, calm, confident, and curious—when the person you are interacting with is operating from their "not-best self" (afraid, angry, judgmental, defensive, and so on). In the absence of consciousness and choice, you get pulled down, and your not-best self and the other's interact. Judgment interacts with judgment. Anger interacts with anger. There is no space for understanding each other in this place. Nothing goods comes of this.

Our reactive tendencies are largely unconscious and a result of feeling threatened. The part of our brain that allows us to think through situations, analyze, and consider gets hijacked, and we very quickly shift to fight, flight, or freeze mode. Lashing out at the driver who cut you off in traffic? Fight. Wanting to hide under your desk rather than deal with an angry colleague? Flight. Completely tongue-tied in the face of a yelling boss? Freeze. You get the picture.

Throughout your career and life, situations will challenge you. You can either react or respond. More accurately, challenges are a daily occurrence. How can you become more conscious and aim to respond? The quote a few pages back, about the difference between reaction and response being ten seconds, is cheeky, yet valid. Time is your friend here. Once we are aware, we can choose.

One way to build awareness is to notice our body sensations. These are quite different when we react immediately versus when we wait to respond. Start noticing for yourself.

For example, when I'm reacting, I stop breathing (not good!), feel like I'm sinking into the floor, have tunnel vision and tightness in my throat, and often want to get the heck out of there (flight); sometimes I want to fight.

When I respond, I feel tall, grounded, clear-minded, and calm, and I take full breaths.

Can you see the huge difference? Our bodies do not lie. They are our barometers that tell us if we are 100 percent ourselves or not. We can either listen to our bodies or ignore them.

I firmly believe that constantly overriding what our bodies are telling us leads to disease, which may manifest in many different ways. This belief stems from my experience as a cancer survivor—I was an elite athlete, ate well, didn't drink, and still got cancer at age thirty-five. I am convinced that my cancer was due, at least in part, to me not having learned how to express and process my emotions and experiences, and instead working really hard to "have it all together" for thirty-five years. It took that long, and getting cancer, for me, a product of my upbringing, to start to work through and learn from my experiences in a healthy way.

Begin to identify the difference between reaction and response by simply becoming aware of the sensations in your body and the feelings associated with them. Try this:

STEP 1: Throughout your day, check in with your physical sensations. Scan your body and notice if any areas pull your attention.

STEP 2: Label the sensation. It might be blue, red, or another color. It might be an animal or another metaphor that applies to it.

STEP 3: Take note of any emotions or thoughts that accompany the sensation. To begin with, don't try to change anything; just note the sensation and accompanying thoughts and emotions, and ask yourself whether you are in reaction or response mode.

By taking the time to check in with your body's sensations, you will develop a buffer from unconscious reactions and create the space to be present to your experience. From there, you'll have the choice to respond in a way that reflects who you are at your best. With this awareness, you can draw on the antidotes for any unconstructive emotions you or another may be feeling. Anger breeds anger. Contempt breeds contempt. Judgment breeds judgment. None of these negative feelings can grow when you come equipped with commitment, generosity, and kindness.

That said, you cannot control the behaviors or attitudes of others. These antidotes may sometimes serve to ground you in who you are so that you can exit a no-win situation with dignity and integrity.

07

A DECENT PROPOSAL

Know Your "No"

Yes, money talks. But it's usually only one of at least five things that matter to people when they're considering a new job proposal. For example, those five things might be family, location, money, health, and friends. Having to compromise on any of your top five may make an offer unappealing. Identify what you'd say yes to and get really clear on when to say no, because a strong "no" makes a "yes" more powerful too.

It was over a decade ago. I had been working at a corporate job for more than four years. It was a large company where I had the opportunity to work in multiple departments. During my time there, I had worked for Smart,

New, Nice, and Wise Bosses. Most weeks, I worked over one hundred hours. I arrived at the office in the very early morning and finished around midnight, then got up and did it all over again. I believed that to stay relevant and get recognized, it was important for me to work these hours, and then work even harder than that.

I never ate breakfast—I had just a handful of almonds for lunch and basically survived on coffee all day long. Years of working like this was taking a toll on me. I had my second baby, and this time I took six weeks off, an eternity compared to my previous mat leave of three days. But it felt like a blink of an eye, and I was back at work in no time.

With a four-year-old and a newborn baby, I was a senior manager working in a new department. I was hired to develop and roll out a global program. It was an exciting project that had an organization-wide impact, taking me to interesting markets; I was testing different methods and techniques, and studying what motivated our employees to go above and beyond for our customers. I managed a small team and was excelling in my role. I made an annual salary of $110,000, which felt like a ton of money on the surface, and yet I was working around the clock. A salary of $110,000 divided by 400 hours per month, or 4,800 hours per year, equals $22 per hour. It was hard to justify the amount of money I was making for the life I was giving up in the process.

My boss was a director and a Nice Boss. I enjoyed working for her; however, I knew I would not continue to grow if I stayed under her for too long. I had already been on her team for a year, which felt like six months too long.

I was told I would be her successor and had worked hard to be seen as that. I had put in the time and made significant sacrifices to demonstrate I was worthy of the director title whenever the job became available. That reality was not far off. Within a few months, my boss announced that she was resigning. I was sad to see her go, yet I was also excited about this new opportunity to step up and fill her shoes. I was ready.

A week went by, then another week, and no one had come to talk to me about the director role. Another week went by: still complete silence. I assumed they just needed time to prepare my offer, and so I waited patiently. A total of four weeks went by, and finally I heard the news—someone else had been assigned the director role and I had been completely overlooked.

I went to the vice-president who hired for this position, and with whom I had a great relationship, to ask him what had happened. Why had I been overlooked for this role? How was it possible? He was shocked and said that the job posting had been up for several weeks and he assumed that if I had wanted it, I would have applied for it. I had no idea the job had been posted and did not know that was the process for being considered for the role. I assumed I would just get promoted.

Literally, within twenty-four hours of my conversation with the VP, I received a job offer from a small, young, nimble company. It was for a director role, but it felt like a big risk and I would have to give up a known commodity for a company I hadn't previously heard of.

I notified my VP of the offer and told him that I had some decisions to make. Little did I know that the choice was about to get even more difficult.

I arrived at work the next day and the VP immediately called me into his office. He offered me the role of director and a $140,000 salary. It was what I had always wanted, and yet there was something about the offer that felt dirty. If I hadn't told him about the other job, would he have proposed this? I thanked him for the offer and let him know I would have to think about it.

An hour later, the senior vice-president (the VP's boss) called me into his office. He sat me down, described what a huge opportunity this was, and said I'd be crazy to not take it. I was honored that someone at such a senior level would take the time to meet with me. And yet, something still felt off, leaving me unable to decide in the moment. I thanked him for taking the time and told him I would think about it.

Within another hour, the VP called me back into his office and offered me more money and an all-expenses-paid education at the executive MBA program at Harvard

Business School. This was a wild offer; it was more than I could have ever asked for.

At the end of the day, I received a request from the CEO to meet him in his office. I had been in meetings with him before, but never one-on-one. He seemed genuinely interested in what was happening and, like the senior VP, talked about the opportunity and the future of the company. He was a very convincing and influential person, with an extremely compelling story. I was sold—I was going to stay and take the role, take the money, and attend Harvard. But... I could not give him a firm answer without talking to my family first. He told me I had one night to think about it and set an 8 a.m. meeting to reconvene on my decision. I was told that no one says no to the CEO, which was fine with me, as I was fully prepared to accept his offer the next day.

I arrived home elated to tell Sean about this exciting day. To my surprise, I was met with sadness. He urged me not to take the role. The sacrifices I had made to get here had taken such a toll on my family that he saw this promotion as a detriment to our happiness and well-being. What it took to get here had nearly ended my marriage and was pulling me further and further apart from my kids.

My stomach was in knots and I was completely torn.

I decided to sleep on it. In the morning, I got ready quickly, made my coffee, and was running out the door to make the early meeting with the CEO. Before leaving,

I peeked into my son's bedroom to find him and my husband lying on the ground, with our German shepherd next to them, having some morning playtime. I remember the moment as if it were yesterday. I asked my son, who was a year old at the time, if we should say yes or no to the offer. Without hesitation, he said, "No." I got a bit teary-eyed and smiled at him, then raced off to my meeting.

As usual, it was a long day and I arrived home very late in the evening. The kids were already asleep and my husband was waiting up for me. He asked me what I told the CEO, almost not wanting to know the answer.

I informed him that I declined the offer.

The relief and the emotions were overwhelming. Years later, I learned that my husband had no idea whether I was going to take the role that morning when I left the house. He had agonized over it all day, not knowing if we'd end up together or apart, based on my decision that day.

A "yes" to the CEO would have been a "no" to my marriage and my family. This simple philosophy made my decision easy and clear.

Get Coached to Work Freely

When we react out of doubt or fear, the emotion is usually fueled by an incorrect and limiting belief or view, which becomes our narrative, causing us to suffer. In the lesson Nancy shared, she was being held by an incorrect belief that if she said no to the work, she'd never get another opportunity. By now you know how strong, resourceful, and talented Nancy is, so that narrative is simply crazy, isn't it? However, to her, it was very real at the time. Think about a time when you made a decision fueled by fear, doubt, or scarcity. *I can't ask for what I want because I'll get fired... I can't ask for help because at my level I should know what to do... He doesn't value my input... She is better than me...*

Such beliefs are holding you hostage. They don't enable you to look at the situation clearly and discern a way forward. You need to be able to see the situation in a different way so that you can make choices that serve you.

"The Work of Byron Katie" is a powerful body of self-inquiry that I often use myself and with clients to question the thoughts and beliefs that hold us back and ultimately cause suffering. Hint: if your thoughts include "should" or "shouldn't," you are likely suffering because you imagine your situation is supposed to be something other than what it is, and you are not accepting what actually is. *I should know how to do that... He should pay me more... It shouldn't be raining... I shouldn't have to do that kind of work... I should have been promoted by now... My partner should appreciate me more...*

"WHEN YOU SAY
YES TO OTHERS,
MAKE SURE YOU
ARE NOT SAYING
NO TO YOURSELF."

PAULO COELHO

Byron Katie's Work is a simple process for exploring and working through the thoughts and beliefs that hold you back. She generously offers it for free online at www.thework.com. I invite you to consider something that you're currently dealing with. Choose a situation with some energy to it that isn't constructive, where you're feeling frustrated, angry, or upset.

Katie breaks down The Work into four steps:

STEP 1. Write down your complaint in a simple statement and then capture all of the judgments and emotions you have about the situation. Don't censor yourself.

EXAMPLE: My direct reports don't respect me.

STEP 2. Get curious about your complaint by answering these four questions:

1 Is it true? (Yes or no. If no, move to question 3.)
2 Can you absolutely know that it's true? (Yes or no.)
3 How do you react—what happens—when you believe that thought?
4 Who would you be without that thought?

Example: Is it true that your direct reports don't respect you? Can you absolutely know that it's true? When I believe that thought, I close off and I stop listening. Without that thought, I would be open to the relationship.

STEP 3. Create turnarounds for the statement.

EXAMPLE: Change your complaint to "I don't respect my direct reports" or "I don't respect myself." Now find examples where these might be true in your interactions with your direct reports. Another turnaround is "My direct reports respect me." Now find examples where that is true.

STEP 4. Embrace reality. After turning around your complaint and exploring the possible "truths," what are you willing to do?

EXAMPLE: I am willing to be vulnerable with my direct reports. I am willing to be transparent. I am willing to ask my direct reports for what I need.

Take these tips for doing The Work:

- Don't censor yourself. If you're pissed off at someone, write it out! Connect with your experience. And then go through the process.
- Use The Work app, available for free online.

FIND YOUR POWER

08

THE VALUE PROPOSITION

Fired or Promoted

If the pull of money, status, or your idea of a "good job" keeps you stuck in a company or with a manager you're not aligned with, you're likely not tasting the sweetness of freedom. This chapter is about getting deeply connected with who you are and crystal clear about the values that ultimately serve as a filter for your work and a foundation for your life.

Defining my values was by far one of the most powerful exercises I have ever done. It has allowed me to operate with strength and clarity every day, to define the choices I make, the company I keep, and what I'm willing to stand up for without fear of the consequences.

"What are you willing

to be fired for?"

In one particular company, I was faced with a circumstance that involved my boss asking me to deploy a large marketing campaign that would hurt the business while my boss would personally and financially benefit.

My initial reaction was anger. I was angry that I would be asked to do this and be put in this position. Then fear set in. This was my boss so if I didn't do it, it would be insubordination and I could be fired. But if I did the marketing campaign, it would unethical. I felt paralyzed.

I had to ask myself what my core values were. My first answer was the core values of the company I worked for, not my personal values. This wasn't right. So I sat down with a piece of blank paper and tried to come up with my own, but the words I wrote were not connecting with me. They were nice words, but they didn't feel authentic. So, for more clarity, I asked one simple question: *What am I willing to be fired for?*

Being fired was my biggest fear and, given the scenario, a reality staring me in the face. And yet, if I had values that were more powerful than my biggest fear, what would they be? The moment I asked myself this question, the answers came naturally, without hesitation: family, freedom, and physical strength.

Was I willing to follow through with the campaign if it meant compromising these three values? The answer was no. If I didn't follow through with the campaign, would I be willing to get fired over it? The answer was hell yeah! Boom! I suddenly was grounded in what would become the most powerful foundation of my life. These were my new parameters.

Family. Freedom. Physical strength.

I had already found difficulties in the job, as I was asked to do things that were incorrect from an academic and functional standard. This was annoying, but in an effort to not rock the boat, I usually nodded my head and obliged. And when I reflected on the job, I saw that quality time with my family was nonexistent. I felt like I was playing small in my career. The circumstances were taking a toll on my energy, leaving me in extreme exhaustion. After work every day, I would fall asleep on the couch at 6 p.m., only to get up in the morning and go through the same grind over again.

Working in conflict with my core values day after day was creating an extreme amount of stress and anxiety. Once I'd clarified my values, it became crystal clear that all three were being compromised. The marketing campaign was the final straw.

Rather than saying no to the unethical campaign ask, I chose to leave the company entirely and, specifically, to leave that boss. He was not Smart, New, Nice, or Wise. He fell outside of the grid and was someone I knew I needed to remove from my path. I left without hesitation and immediately found balance with my core values.

"IT'S ONLY BY SAYING

'NO' THAT YOU CAN

CONCENTRATE ON

THE THINGS THAT ARE

REALLY IMPORTANT."

STEVE JOBS

Since then, I have encountered a handful of similar situations and applied my core value filter each time. Decisions became easier and put me in control of my own destiny. They are part of my personal identity—people know they can count on me to always stand up for what's right instead of taking the easy route.

These three values are authentically mine. They have deep meaning in my life and influence my actions on a daily basis. They are my strategic pillars, the three things I must always have in balance in order to be my best, most powerful self. When they are out of whack, I lose my footing and give up my power.

Living your life without core values is like paddling a rudderless boat. You might be moving, but you are likely not moving with purpose. Defining your values will give more meaning to your work, make difficult decisions easier, and lend clarity to your actions in the face of challenges.

Get Coached to Work Freely

How present are you to your values? How intentional are you in making choices that align with your values? How intentional have you been in the past? A litmus test is the degree to which your choices and actions led you to fulfillment, engagement, presence, and strength—or frustration, fatigue, smallness, and inauthenticity. (If you are new to the idea of core values or want to review yours, go to chapter 4.)

Let's normalize this. We are all humans having a human experience, which includes, at times, overriding what we know is best—what our inner self tells us—and making decisions based on our fears, doubts, and shoulds. Our core values are true to us and always available to us. Put in place structures that enable you to quickly connect with those values, that which is authentically you.

Here are some ideas:

FOR THE ANALYTICAL: Create a checklist of questions to ask yourself when making a decision and rate how well the decision would reflect what is most important for you on a scale of 1 to 10 (with 1 indicating that it's a low priority and 10 indicating a high priority).

FOR THE VISIONARIES: Fill in the blank: I have made the decision to _____. Then look ten years, or perhaps just one week, into the future. In the eyes of your wise and knowing self, what is happening? How are you feeling? Are you operating at your best?

FOR THE CONNECTORS: Engage those who know you best—those who hold the vision of who you truly are and won't get derailed by your shoulds or sabotaging thoughts—and ask them how well your choice of Path X or Path Y would reflect who you are.

FOR THE REFLECTORS: Take a minute. A day. A week. Consider what you really want. Create a Power of Knowing What You Want drawing for this issue (see chapter 2). How does this fit into your vision?

09
A FANCY TITLE

Know Your People

A title, a level, and letters after your name confer a lot of pride. And yet without these qualifiers, you're still the same person, just without a label. Stripping back the things that give us a false sense of power leaves us vulnerable, naked, and real. A grand sense of freedom comes when you take power into your own hands and surround yourself with people who support you in determining your worth, value, and limitless potential to design a life you love.

At lululemon, we often asked ourselves, "If you knew you couldn't fail, what would you do?" The answer to this often led to powerful leadership and bold moves. I was happy at my job and had recently been promoted to vice-president. I had reached my goal, and yet when I got the promotion, I still felt like something was missing, as if I was playing small.

If I wasn't afraid, what would I do?

Answer: I would quit my job and join a pre-revenue start-up. I wanted to be part of a founding team and build a brand from scratch. Sure enough, the universe delivered.

I was recruited to be the chief marketing officer of a health tech start-up. It took me several months to assess the opportunity and make sure I could afford the risk. When I finally decided to give notice, I felt strong, courageous, and fearless; I was excited. The opportunity and the adventure felt enormous. I could not wait for the next chapter. After five years at lululemon, I left my job without hesitation.

The company I went to was dynamic, with brilliant people from well-known, established brands who were brought together to launch a modern, innovative, and fashionable product that had the capacity to save millions of lives. The company was the one of the highest venture capital–backed start-ups, having closed a $20 million funding round just months prior to my arrival.

However, there was a problem. The company was burning so much money on supporting a large team and endless testing and trials that, within six months, it ran out of cash and folded.

Because of this, everyone in the company was let go. I remember that day. My worst fear of being fired had become a reality. I walked calmly into the office, quietly gathered my things, and walked to the meeting room that had been set up the day before. I sat there for about an hour, waiting for my turn, watching as each person on the team was let go.

When they finally called my name, I sat quietly as they formally read the terms of my separation. I took the paperwork and walked out somewhat relieved that it was over. While feeling drained and directionless, I had survived one of my worst fears and was still standing.

The following few days were like vacation. I did all the things I never had time for, like spending an hour at the neighborhood drugstore buying a basketful of makeup and shampoo. Or walking up and down every single aisle in Costco filling up my cart with hundreds of dollars of items I never knew I needed, not forgetting to complete my experience with a hot dog and soda before leaving the premises.

I reorganized my entire kitchen, worked out like a fiend, and became a master snack maker, preparing the fanciest homemade snacks so they'd be ready and waiting for my kids to walk in the door and devour them.

And yet, within a few days, the fun began to fade. Reality hit me like a ton of bricks. I had nowhere to go each day, no real purpose, and I had completely lost my identity overnight. I always associated my self-worth with the brand I worked for and the title I was given. And for the first time in my career, I was just Nancy. But who was that?

People came out of the

woodwork when I needed

them the most. Some had

been in my life recently, and

others were there no matter

how much time had passed

since our last interaction—

all there unconditionally.

I remember sitting on the couch as my kids walked out the door to catch the school bus. They had their routine, and I was supposed to go to work. The calendar invites stopped, I did not have a single email, and for the first time I was free—and yet I felt anything but free.

I was embarrassed and sad. I stayed home for weeks in order to avoid running into anyone I knew because I didn't want to explain why I wasn't at work. I feared being introduced to people because I'd be asked what I do. My title had always been my identity—they were one in the same—but I didn't have an answer I was proud of.

Later, as I looked back at this time and recalled how anxious, insecure, and uncertain I felt about what I would do next, it was obvious who stood by my side even when I had nothing to offer. These were my people.

The people who still accepted a coffee date even though I couldn't offer them a job or a promotion. The people who still gave me an outstanding reference even when there was no payout for them. The people who still believed in my potential even when I had lost all hope for myself. If they are reading this, they know who they are.

To my surprise, this group of people was significantly smaller after I lost my job than when I had a fancy brand and title. But certain people stuck by my side that I did not anticipate.

This period in my life taught me two valuable lessons:

1. LESS IS MORE. When going through challenging times, it's important to shrink your circle to those who lift you up and serve as a positive force in your recovery.

2. YOU ARE NOT YOUR TITLE. Success is a feeling; it is not tied to a job or a fancy title. Those would come and go, but they did not define me.

Get Coached to Work Freely

You are not your title.

You are not your salary.

You are not how you look.

You are not your fastest 10K or marathon or Ironman time.

You are not the number of your Facebook and Instagram followers.

You are not defined by how "busy" you are.

When you live a big life, take risks, and set big goals, you will sometimes fail. You will take on a huge role with a start-up and the funding may run out. You will move to a new country with the love of your life and the relationship may not work out. You will train for the Boston Marathon and may tear your ACL two weeks before the race. There are no guarantees.

"STOP ACTING SO
SMALL. YOU ARE
THE UNIVERSE IN
ECSTATIC MOTION."

RUMI

Lululemon's goal-setting philosophy, which Nancy and I continue to practice, is that if you're not failing in 50 percent of your goals, then the goals are simply not big enough. Going big means you will experience times when you don't achieve your objectives. This does not make you a failure. It does not make you less of a person. It does not mean you are less worthy. It's quite the opposite. Here's another way of looking at it. You may not hit your goal 100 percent; however, you will have learned so much in the process and you will be fundamentally further ahead than if you had never tried in the first place. The gift is learning. Nancy, in choosing to leave lululemon for a new job, learned how resilient she was. While she might have momentarily seen losing the job as a failure, Nancy came to see that failing at something didn't make *her* a failure. Then she noticed all the people around her who were there to support her as she developed her next move.

Take the time to consider six simple questions:

1 If you knew you could not fail and those around you would not only suspend judgment but would whole-heartedly support you, what would you do?
2 Are you doing it?
3 If not, why?
4 If your reason for not doing it is that you are afraid of failing or being judged, how much worse would it be to regret never even trying?

5 If it did fail, what's the worst that could happen? What is the very worst? And how could you deal with it?

6 Who will wholeheartedly support you, no matter what? Those are your people.

The fact is that you are infinitely resourceful. You have dealt with failures, setbacks, and disappointments in the past. Our fear of failing is often much greater than the actual consequences would be, which sadly holds us back from leaning into our dreams and goals. Shift your relationship with failure. Failure is a gift to learn from, not something to be avoided and feared. Bring it on!

10

SUPER SELF

Release Your Gravity

It takes the failures to appreciate the wins. And yet, when failures hit, suddenly life can feel uncertain and finding the motivation to persevere insurmountable. But you can access a new dimension of yourself, one with limitless potential that's capable of anything. This inner force will help you define where you're going and what you need to do to overcome what holds you back.

I believe deeply in the process of goal setting. At the end of every year, I spend anywhere from a few hours to a few weeks preparing my goals for the upcoming year. I am usually rushed and find myself quickly jotting down thoughts in a notebook or on scrap paper.

However, at the end of one particular year, I found myself at a crossroads. I worked for someone who threatened to ruin my career if I ever left him. I was scared, but I knew I could not let fear guide my decisions. His abusive nature had become so bad that I could no longer be a bystander. It was another defining moment in which I had to ask myself if I was willing to give up my job to do the right thing. Would I stand up and fight or exit quietly and leave it for someone else to deal with?

I chose to stand up and fight.

He was ultimately held accountable, but I still felt anything but free. The process had taken such a toll on me over several months that I finally decided to leave. It was a purposeful departure, but I still had stayed too long under an abusive boss. My confidence was so beaten down, I started to doubt myself.

I needed a break and was burnt out. I spent a couple of months on the couch. I call this my "back door"—the place I go to hide. It was a comfortable couch made of soft, cushiony denim that sucked you right in. I had a thick gray comforter that I'd throw on top of me, and between the two, it was like getting a big warm hug that I never wanted to end. I didn't leave the house for weeks, and I made a point to not talk to anyone except my family and a couple of close friends—only my people. It was a safe place to live, but life was at a standstill.

Eventually, I realized that it was time for a change. I needed to dig deep and find a renewed sense of purpose.

I decided to get a room for two nights at the Fairmont Hotel. I needed to find a neutral, comfortable space where I could clear my head and begin to set new goals.

When I arrived in the room, I pulled out a blank piece of paper and wrote down three declarations:

1   I don't work simply to make money.
2   I work for a bigger purpose that is in line with my core values.
3   I work with people with whom there is mutual respect.

Then I wrote down "things to preserve" that were working for me:

- family
- physical strength
- freedom
- developing teams
- daily commitments
- vulnerability
- humility
- resilience
- humor
- guts

And then I made a list of "things to change" that were not serving me:

- caring what others think
- defensiveness
- schedules
- playing small

I spent the next twenty-four hours writing my one-, three-, and five-year goals. I acknowledged the things that would contribute to my success in achieving these goals:

- friends
- coaches
- family
- mentors
- dog (of course)
- fitness
- forest walks
- lack of ego
- fearlessness
- gratitude
- patience

My stay at the hotel was coming to an end. I was excited about my new goals, and yet something still felt very off. In my head, I knew what I had to do, but my body felt disconnected. My stomach hurt, I was irritable, and my heart physically ached. I left the hotel that day feeling uneasy, as if my work was incomplete.

On my way home, I had to stop for an osteopathy appointment that had been on my calendar for months. I'm not one to see a doctor, ever, but on this particular day, I decided a little self-care couldn't hurt. Located in a tiny office in the heart of Vancouver was my osteopath, whom I called my "witch doctor." She is beautiful, young, and smart with long hair, a gentle smile, and eyes that reveal an old soul. I shared with her the goals I was excited about, but I also told her that I still felt deeply wounded inside. She gently worked on me for ninety minutes. At the end of the session, she said my heart, my spine, and my head were not aligned. And in a very matter-of-fact tone, she told me to just lie low and I would start to feel better within a few days.

She was right.

Within several days, I felt great. I had my goals on a page, my body felt strong, and I was prepared to pull myself off the couch and get after it. However, I had one final phase of goal setting I had not acknowledged yet.

My gravity.

I had been out for drinks with a colleague of mine a few years prior and he had mentioned the importance of identifying your gravity whenever you feel stuck. In my situation, I realized that I needed to acknowledge and identify my gravity so that I could release the things that were holding me back.

I pulled out a blank piece of paper and started writing:

- fear of failure
- self-doubt
- bullies
- guilt
- fear of rejection

This list represented my gravity. The items came to me so easily. Each one represented a heavy weight on my shoulders.

The fear of failure, bookended with the fear of rejection, was a powerful force that led me to opt out of opportunities. If I interviewed for a job, I'd find a reason to back out before they could say no. If I invited someone out to dinner, I would give them every excuse to decline. It is called self-sabotage, and it is one of my greatest gifts, rooted in the fear of failure and rejection. In order to release my gravity, I had to counteract each one with a new declaration:

FEAR OF FAILURE/"I am afraid to fail."
New declaration: Let go of what other people think. Their view of my success is a reflection of what they believe success is for themselves.

SELF-DOUBT/"I doubt I can do it."
New declaration: Let go of the past. Stop thinking about what could have been, and focus on what I'm going to do next.

BULLIES/"I give up my power to bullies."
New declaration: I choose to surround myself with people who share my values.

GUILT/"I feel bad about what happened."
New declaration: The path I've chosen is powerful and will lead me to a better place.

FEAR OF REJECTION/"I'm worried they will say no."
New declaration: When one door closes, another will open.

When gravity takes hold, my natural inclination is to remove myself, back out of opportunities, and retreat to my warm, comfortable couch. The beautiful thing is that when you know this, you can acknowledge your gravity and make new declarations to let it go. From there, anything is possible.

Whenever I feel I've lost my footing or I'm lacking a sense of direction, I use this tool to sort through thoughts, feelings, and pain points to keep me on the path of working freely. Because when you work freely, you love your life. And when you love your life, you do phenomenal work. And when you do phenomenal work, the opportunities are endless and creating a life you love is not just possible—it is a sure thing.

To help with this process, download the goal-setting worksheet at www.workfreely.co.

Get Coached to Work Freely

We all experience what Nancy calls gravity. It is part of being human. Through our life experiences, we accumulate limiting thoughts and beliefs that are actually incorrect and lead us to playing small and feeling unfulfilled. It's time to let go of what's holding you down and soar in the direction of your purpose, your goals, your dreams.

How do you manage your gravity, those beliefs and/ or perspectives that hold you down? By putting on your metaphorical superhero cape so you can fly. That cape connects with that part of yourself that knows who you are and what you're capable of. I refer to that part of you as your Super Self. You may have heard it described as your wise self, inner guide, sage, or captain. Call it whatever makes sense for you. Your Super Self is an internal guide, the leader within you, the wise part that leads you to the fullest expression of your values, your purpose, your destiny. Your Super Self is the grounding force that knows what's needed and how to proceed in any situation. Your Super Self is badass—fearless, courageous, unstoppable,

"YOU WILL FIND YOUR TRUTH MORE QUICKLY THROUGH DELIGHT THAN GRAVITY. LET A LITTLE MORE STRING OUT ON YOUR KITE."

ALAN COHEN

and always loyal to you (not your saboteur). Here's the kicker: your Super Self is always a part of you and is always, always available.

Nancy was able to create positive declarations to lift herself out of her gravity by connecting with that part of herself that knows who she is at her core—her infinite resourcefulness, wisdom, and courage. She connected to her Super Self.

The key is to get to know this part of you so you can connect with your Super Self whenever and wherever you need to.

You may already have a visualization practice that allows you to go inward with intention and inquiry. If not, consider trying on the following one. I recommend reading through the exercise a couple of times so that you can then experience the visualization without having to read it. Or you may ask someone you trust to take you through the visualization. You can also allow us to take you through this guided visualization. The MP3 version is available on www.workfreely.co.

Guided Visioning to Meet Your Super Self

Find a quiet space where you will be uninterrupted. This could be inside or outside in nature. The key is to be with just yourself for up to twenty minutes. No distractions.

Find a comfortable position you can relax in for a short journey to meet your Super Self.

Take a slow deep breath through your nose, and as you release that breath, let yourself relax. Notice where you might hold tension... Breathe into that place and let go of that tension on the exhale. Another breath now, letting go of any remaining tension... As you relax, let your mind wander to a place that is completely safe... Just make it up, sense it, or see it. You are in a place that feels comfortable, happy, safe... As you imagine this place, take the time to look around. What do you notice? What are you paying attention to? What do you see? Hear? Smell? Whatever you see, imagine or sense it exactly as it should be. Take in the colors, the sounds... You might want to touch something. What are the smells here? Let it all come so alive for you...

As you settle into this space, you hear the sound of someone approaching. There is a sense of knowing and anticipation in the air. You are about to meet someone special. And now, they come into view. Your Super Self walks toward you, excited to meet you as well.

As your Super Self approaches, take the time to notice and appreciate. What does your Super Self look like? What is the energy like? What stands out to you about them? What's it like being with your Super Self? Allow enough time for answers to come.

This is the leader within you, your inner guide. Greet each other. Notice what it's like. Your Super Self has always been here, and now you have access to each other in a new and conscious way.

Now, it's time to learn from your Super Self. Make sure you are comfortable in this safe space. Take your time to ask them the following questions and listen carefully for the answers:

1 What is important for me to know about you? (*pause*)
2 What do you want for me? (*pause*)
3 What limiting beliefs do you want me to let go of? (*pause*)
4 What do you know about my life's purpose? (*pause*)
5 How can I connect easily with you, your wisdom, and your strength? (*pause*)
6 What name shall I call you? (*pause*)
7 What else do you want me to ask you? (*pause*)

Once you've completed these questions, you see that your Super Self has a gift for you. Receive it. What is the gift? What do you notice about it? Ask your Super Self: *What is the importance of this gift? How do you want me to use it?*

Notice how you are feeling in this moment. Notice what it is like to be with this part of you. You'll now bring this time together to a close. It's time to thank each other, knowing that you now have a way to easily connect with your Super Self at any time, in service of you living your life on purpose.

Take a deep breath, breathing in this experience, remembering what you need to remember. Another breath, returning to this space and time... another deep breath. Open your eyes, stretch, move your body.

Capture any notes about this experience in a journal.

Congratulations! You now have access to your Super Self, the part of you that is much stronger and fiercer than your gravity. Don't let it end here. Make the time going forward to get to know your Super Self and determine ways for you to quickly and easily access that part of you. Your Super Self always has your back.

WHAT'S NEXT?

THIS BOOK IS about choosing your life, defining your leadership, and finding your power. Depending on where you are at in your life and what challenges you're facing, each story and coaching session will read and sound different. Use this book as a tool to fall back on, as an ongoing resource for when you encounter challenges that compromise your freedom in the workplace. We also invite you to continue the conversation by joining our Work Freely online community, where you can ask questions, get help finding a coach, share your own stories, and read those of others at www.workfreely.co.

THANKS

THANK YOU TO our many colleagues and friends from lululemon athletica, as well as Susanne Conrad from Lightyear Leadership, for teaching us how to be leaders in the world; our husbands for supporting us throughout this journey; and our four-legged pups for your unconditional love.

ABOUT THE AUTHORS

Nancy Richardson

Wife, mom, and dedicated student of Muay Thai kick-boxing and Brazilian jiujitsu, Nancy Richardson began her career with a BA from the University of Washington and an MBA from Ohio State University. After more than twenty years of working in large, corporate environments, including Starbucks and lululemon—where she put in insane hours, had little time with her family, and felt others determined her worth—she decided to design her own life by tapping into the era of start-ups and passion projects, building meaningful brands, and working from home to spend more time with her family.

Nancy is the Co-Founder and Principal Strategist of Dragon Lady and Mom 'n' Pop Shop, two women-led, Vancouver-based marketing start-ups that embody the concept of working freely. Her mission is to embolden the workforce of the future.

Nancy was born and raised in Honolulu, Hawaii, and currently lives in Vancouver, Canada.

Rochelle Davidson

Rochelle Davidson is a wife, mom to rescue dogs, endurance cyclist, adventure traveler, and passionate executive coach and leadership development practitioner. With a BA in Business from the University of British Columbia and an MA in Applied Behavioral Sciences from Bastyr University, Rochelle is at her best when partnering with leaders to create healthy workplaces and to get results that matter.

Rochelle's life was rocked when, in 2005, she heard the words "You've got cancer." Her personal experience further fueled her mission to see people and organizations thrive, not merely survive. She supports her clients in creating environments where their people are inspired, connect to each other in meaningful ways, and use their strengths to contribute to something bigger than themselves, taking their best selves to their families, friends, and communities at the end of the day. She has worked with global companies such as lululemon athletica, Accenture, and Crystal Decisions. Rochelle is a certified professional coach, credentialed through the International Coach Federation and Coaches Training Institute.

Rochelle was born, raised, and lives a life she loves, in Vancouver, Canada. Visit www.rochelledavidson.com.

CPSIA information can be obtained
at www.ICGtesting.com
Printed in the USA
FSHW011831010919
61645FS